Compensatory Education Program

finding out about
SIMPLE MACHINES

By GENE DARBY
Supervisor and Teacher
Redding, California

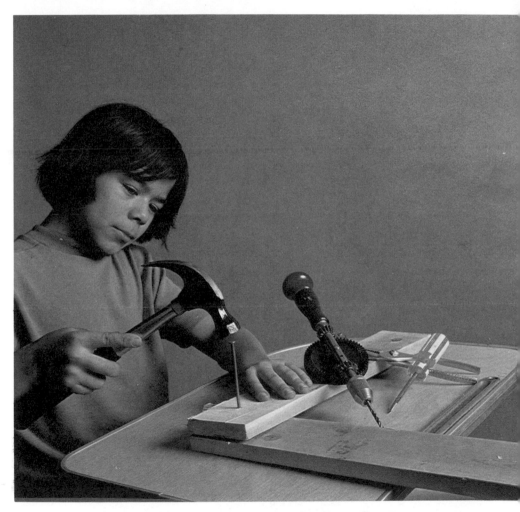

Benefic Press • Westchester, Illinois

finding out about

Living Things
finding out about ANIMALS
finding out about PLANTS
finding out about BIRDS
finding out about FISH

Matter and Energy
finding out about SOLIDS, LIQUIDS, AND GASES
finding out about SIMPLE MACHINES
finding out about WEATHER
finding out about MAGNETS

Earth and the Universe
finding out about SEASONS
finding out about THE EARTH
finding out about THE SUN AND MOON
finding out about ECOLOGY

Filmstrips, Cassette, and Experiment Cards
available for each title

Copyright 1974 by Benefic Press
All Rights Reserved
Printed in the United States of America

Library of Congress
Number 73-86786
ISBN 0-8175-7431-X

CONTENTS

Simple machines can be found all around us.

Do you know what a simple machine is? Do you know what simple machines you use?

People use many simple machines to make machines like this one.

4

Can you find the simple machines in this machine?

Simple machines help people do work.

Do you know what work is? Do you know how a simple machine helps people do work?

You can find out.

THE SIMPLE MACHINES

These are the six simple machines.

They are the pulley, the wedge, the wheel and axle, the inclined plane, the lever, and the screw.

Each simple machine can be found in many other machines.

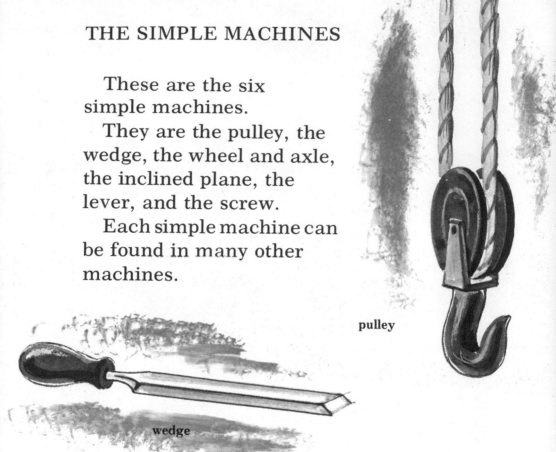

pulley

wedge

inclined plane

6

wheel and axle

Some machines lift things, while others push things apart.

Some machines help people go up to high places easily.

screw

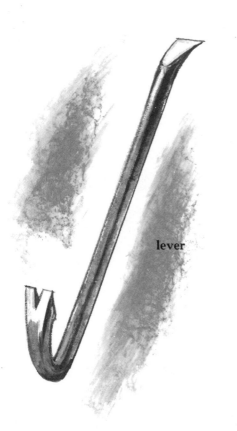

lever

These machines help people do some kind of work. Do you know what work is?

7

Work is moving something from one place to another place.

Perhaps you want to move a box. You try very hard, but the box will not move. You pull and pull, but you cannot move the box at all.

You feel as though you have worked hard. But you have not done work, because the box did not move.

Then you have a good idea. You will make wheels and axles for the box.

Maybe they can help.

You put the wheels and axles on the box and try to move it.

Now the box will move. You have done work.

Some simple machines help people lift very heavy things. Simple machines can help you break a stone apart, or open a can of juice.

Some machines
help people load
boxes into trucks.

Some simple
machines can help
you fix a toy.

Some simple
machines can help
people raise a flag.

THE LEVER

These are levers.
A lever is usually
a hard bar that is
used to move things.
Levers are found
in many shapes.

Levers help people
lift heavy boxes, pull
nails, loosen screws,
and row boats.
Levers work in
different ways, but all
levers can help
people to do work.

All levers need three things to work. They need a load, a fulcrum, and a force.

The load is the thing the lever moves. The force is what moves the lever. The fulcrum is the place where the lever rests. The load and the force move, and the fulcrum stays in the same place.

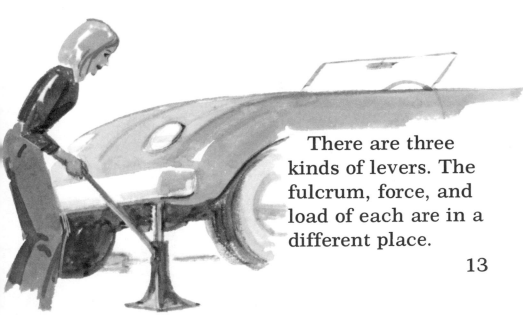

There are three kinds of levers. The fulcrum, force, and load of each are in a different place.

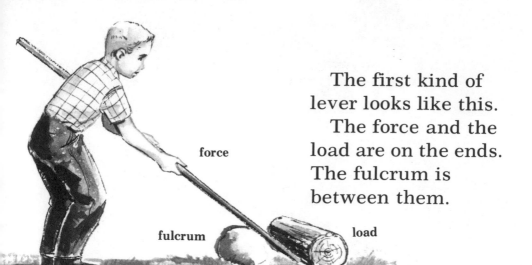

The first kind of
lever looks like this.
The force and the
load are on the ends.
The fulcrum is
between them.

force

fulcrum

load

When someone pushes down on one end of
the stick, the log goes up on the other end. The
hands pushing down are the force, the log is
the load, and the rock where the lever rests is
the fulcrum.

14

This is the second kind
of lever. The force and
fulcrum are on the ends.
The load is between them.

The hands are the force.
The dog is the load. The axle
of the wheel is the fulcrum.
When someone lifts the
handles, the load goes up.

15

This is the third kind of lever.
The fulcrum and the load are on the ends, with the force between them.

force

fulcrum

load

The fish is the load. The place where the pole rests is the fulcrum. The hands show where the force is.

When someone lifts the pole, the load goes up, too.

16

Find out which lever will lift a load with the least force.
You will need these.

Make a chart like this one.

Make a lever like the first kind on the chart. Move the lever on the fulcrum, as the chart shows. How much force is needed each time?

Make a lever like the second kind on the chart. Move the load this time, as the chart shows. How much force is needed each time?

Make a lever like the third kind on the chart. Move the force this time. How much force do you need?

Which lever needed the least force? Which needed the most?

What kind of lever are these things? Are they the first, second, or third kind? How do you know?

Where are the fulcrum, load, and force in each of these levers?

THE WHEEL AND AXLE

This simple machine
is a wheel and axle.

An axle is a bar going through the middle
of the wheel. The wheel turns on the axle.
Sometimes, the axle turns with the wheel.
This machine helps people move things.

A wheel is like a
part of a roller.

A roller moves like
a wheel. But a roller
will not stay under
the thing you want to
move.

An axle can hold
the wheel in place.

This kind of wheel
and axle is a gear.
A gear is round,
but its edge is not
smooth.
A gear has teeth all
around its edge.

The teeth of a gear
fit the teeth of other
gears. When one
turns, the others
turn, too.

A gear may change
the way other gears
turn, like this

or like this.

21

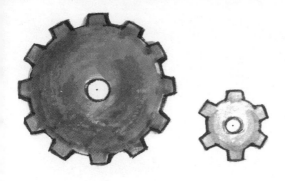

This small gear
turns faster than the
large one.

This gear has six
teeth around its
edge.

This gear has
twelve teeth around
its edge.

When the large gear turns around once,
the small gear goes around two times.

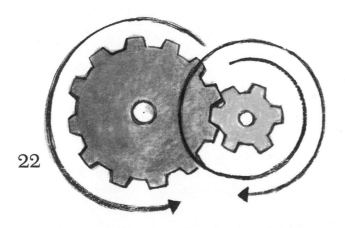

22

The teeth of a gear
do not have to meet
the teeth of another
gear to move it.

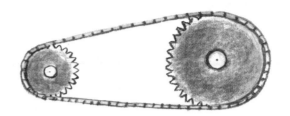

A chain that goes
over the teeth of a
gear can move it.

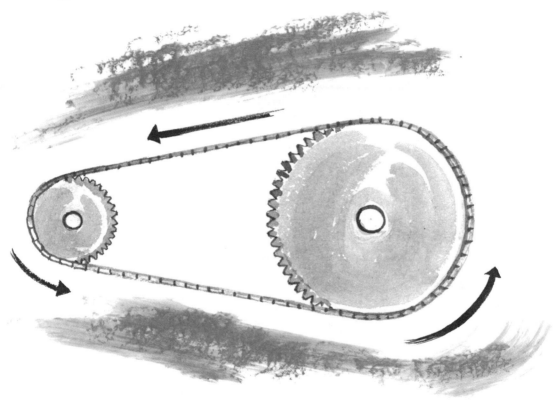

When a chain is used, the gears move the
same way.

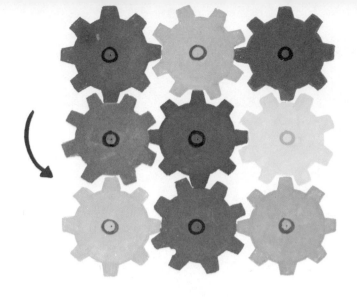

The way one gear will
turn is shown here. How
will the other gears turn?

How many times
will the small gear
turn if you turn the
large gear once?

THE PULLEY

This is a pulley.
A pulley looks like a wheel and axle, but it is different in two ways.

A pulley has an edge like this. It is made this way so a rope will fit and not fall off the wheel.

Pulleys, like wheels, have axles, but their axles never turn.
The wheel turns, but the axle stays in the same place.

25

This is one kind of pulley.

It is called a fixed pulley because it does not have to move to help move other things.

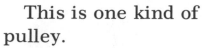

The wheel turns, but the whole pulley stays in the same place all the time.

With this kind of pulley, the thing you want to move hangs on the rope, not on the pulley.

This is another
kind of pulley.

This kind of pulley
has to move to help
move other things.

This kind is called
a movable pulley.

With this kind of
pulley, the thing you
want to move hangs
from the pulley, not
from the rope.

People can use fixed and movable pulleys together to make a machine called a block and tackle.

It is used to lift very heavy things.

It has one pulley that does not move.

It has one pulley that does move.

The load is here.

A block and tackle can lift heavier things than one pulley alone, because two ropes hold up the load. Here ropes B and C hold the load.

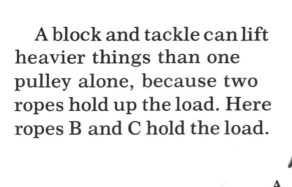

When rope A is pulled, the fixed pulley turns. Rope B is pulled through this pulley.

When rope B is pulled up, the movable pulley turns.

Rope C is pulled through the movable pulley, and the load is lifted off the ground.

29

This is another kind of
block and tackle.

It uses two fixed pulleys
and two movable pulleys.

Find the fixed pulleys.

Find the movable pulleys.

Pulleys can be
used in many ways.
They can be used
to lift things up.

They can be used
to pull things across
from one place to
another.

They can be used
like this in a car.

Find out how pulleys can help people lift heavy things easily. You will need these.

Tie a pulley to a chair. Pull a string through the pulley. Tie it to a book. Use a scale to find how much force will lift the book.

Tie the string to the chair. Tie the book to a pulley. Use the scale to find how much force will lift the book.

Make a block and tackle like this one. How much force will lift the book when you use two pulleys like this?

Make a block and tackle like this one. How much force do you need now? Which pulley lifted the book most easily? Why do you think so?

THE INCLINED PLANE

An inclined plane
is used for moving
things to a high place
without having to lift
them up. One end is
higher than the other
end. It is flat.

An inclined plane
helps people get down
from high places, too.
These inclined
planes help people
get down safely.

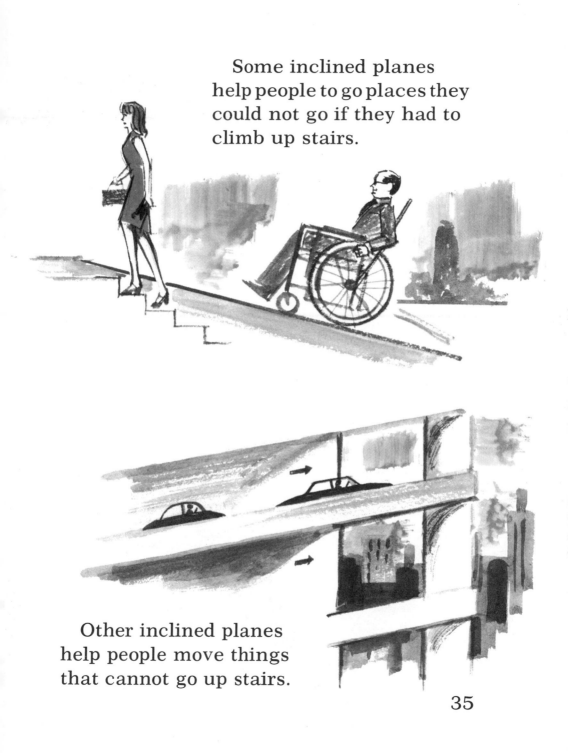

Some inclined planes
help people to go places they
could not go if they had to
climb up stairs.

Other inclined planes
help people move things
that cannot go up stairs.

Inclined planes are used by cars and trains to get up hills or across rivers.

THE WEDGE

This simple machine is a wedge.
The wedge is really two inclined planes, back to back.

All wedges have an edge
that cuts through, or is
pushed through something.

Many wedges are used with a lever, like a nail with a hammer.

Wedges can be a part of a lever, like an ax.

Can you find the lever that has a wedge?

39

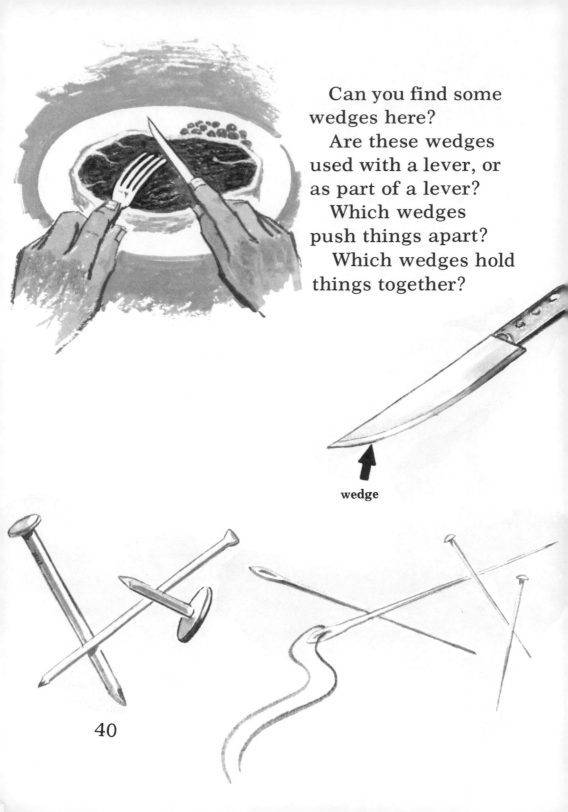

Can you find some wedges here?

Are these wedges used with a lever, or as part of a lever?

Which wedges push things apart?

Which wedges hold things together?

wedge

THE SCREW

A screw pushes things
together and holds them.

It is used to help people
push up very heavy things.

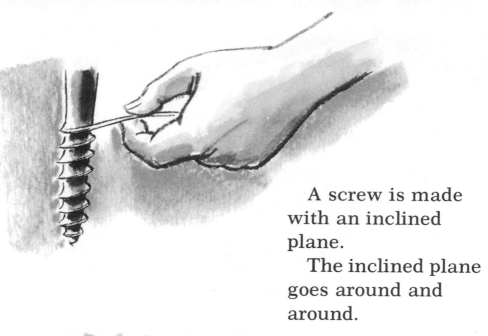

A screw is made
with an inclined
plane.

The inclined plane
goes around and
around.

You can see how this is done.
Cut the shape of an inclined
plane from paper, and roll
the paper around a pencil. It
will look like this.

Some screws have
a point, or a wedge.

Others do not have
any point.

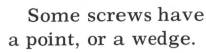

Some screws are
used with what you
are holding together.

Others need a
piece of metal, called
a nut, to work.

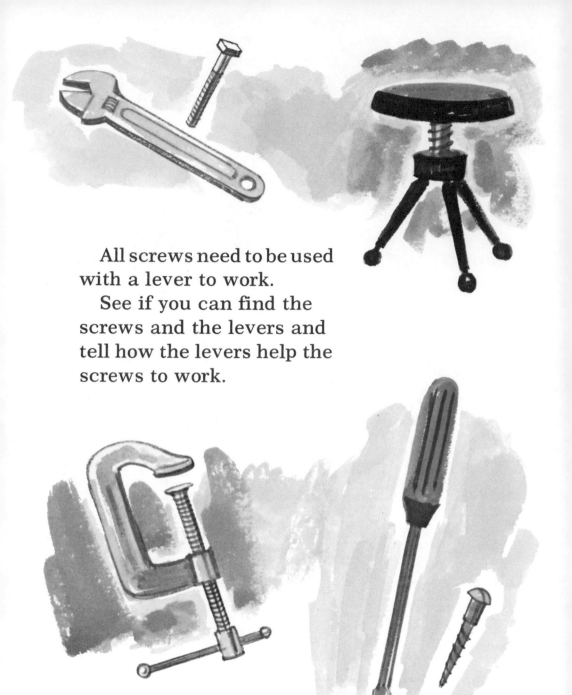

All screws need to be used
with a lever to work.

See if you can find the
screws and the levers and
tell how the levers help the
screws to work.

    People can put these simple machines
together to make a different machine.

    A machine that is made from more than one
simple machine is called a complex machine.

    Look at this pair of scissors.

    How many simple machines can you find in
this complex machine?

    Can you see the lever, wedge, and screw?

45

Look at these machines.
All of these machines
have simple machines in
them.
    How many can you find?

Simple machines are all around us.

You use many of them every day. When you open a door, play ball, raise the flag, open a can of juice, or ride a bicycle, you are using some kind of simple machine.

What do you think the world would be like without simple machines?

PICTURE DICTIONARY

A LEVER is a hard bar used for moving things. It has a force, a fulcrum, and a load. There are three kinds of levers.

A SCREW is a bar with an inclined plane going around it. It pushes things together and holds them.

A WHEEL AND AXLE is a wheel with a bar in the middle. The wheel can turn on the axle, or the axle can turn with the wheel.

A PULLEY is like a wheel and axle, but it has a different edge, made so a rope will fit. It also has an axle which never turns.

A WEDGE is two inclined planes. Wedges push things apart, or cut through things.

The reading vocabulary of this book is at the second grade level.

ACKNOWLEDGMENTS

Illustrations:	James Teason
Photos:	Photography Unlimited (pages 1, 17, and 32)
	Bill Jirkovsky (pages 4-5)
Cover:	Norman Herlihy (design)
	Product Illustration, Inc. (art work)

Demonstrations found on pages 7-8, 22, 29, and 42.
Experiments found on pages 17 and 32.
Detailed explanation of these experiments available in the film-strips **Finding Out About Simple Machines: Experiment 1** and **Finding Out About Simple Machines: Experiment 2.**